IN A People House

By **Dr. Seuss***

*writing as
Theo. LeSieg

Illustrated by *Roy McKie*

A Bright and Early Book
From BEGINNER BOOKS®
A Division of Random House, Inc.

Published in the United States by Random House Children's Books, a division of
Random House, Inc., New York.

BRIGHT AND EARLY BOOKS and colophon and RANDOM HOUSE and colophon are registered
trademarks of Random House, Inc.

www.randomhouse.com/kids
www.seussville.com

Educators and librarians, for a variety of teaching tools, visit us at www.randomhouse.com/teachers

Library of Congress Cataloging-in-Publication Data:
Seuss, Dr. In a people house. (A Bright and early book, #12)
SUMMARY: Easy-to-read rhyme cites a number of common household items.
[1. Stories in rhyme.] I. McKie, Roy, illus.
II. Title. PZ8.3S477In 398.8 [E] 75-37406
ISBN: 978-0-394-82395-9 (trade) — ISBN: 978-0-394-92395-6 (lib. bdg.)

Printed in the United States of America

"Come inside, Mr. Bird,"
said the mouse.
"I'll show you what there is
in a People House . . . .

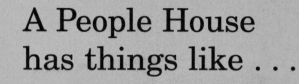

A People House
has things like . . .

. . . chairs

things like
roller skates

and stairs.

banana

bathtub

bottles

brooms

That's what you find
in people's rooms.

scissors

needle

buttons

thread

cup
and
saucer

pillow

bed

These are doughnuts.

Here's
a
door.

Come along, I'll show you more.

Here's a
ceiling

here's a floor

piano

peanuts

popcorn

pails

pencil

paper

hammer

nails

salt and pepper

goldfish

key

table

telephone

TV

Come on!
Come on!
There's more to see!

You'll see a
kitchen sink
in a People House,

a shoe

and a sock

and a clock

said the mouse.

bread **and** butter

window

wall

toothbrush

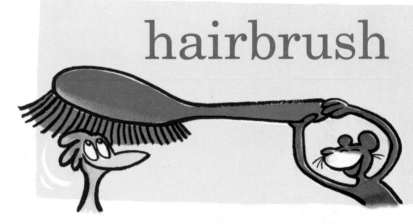

hairbrush

big blue ball

baked beans

bureau drawers

and

books

lights and lamps

and hats and hooks

mirror

marbles

shirt

and string

knife

fork

spoon

and

bells

to

ring

doll

and

dishes

teapot

trash

And . . .
Another thing,
it's time
you knew . . .

. . . A People House
has people, too!

"And now, Mr. Bird,
you know," said the mouse.
"You know what there is
in a People House."

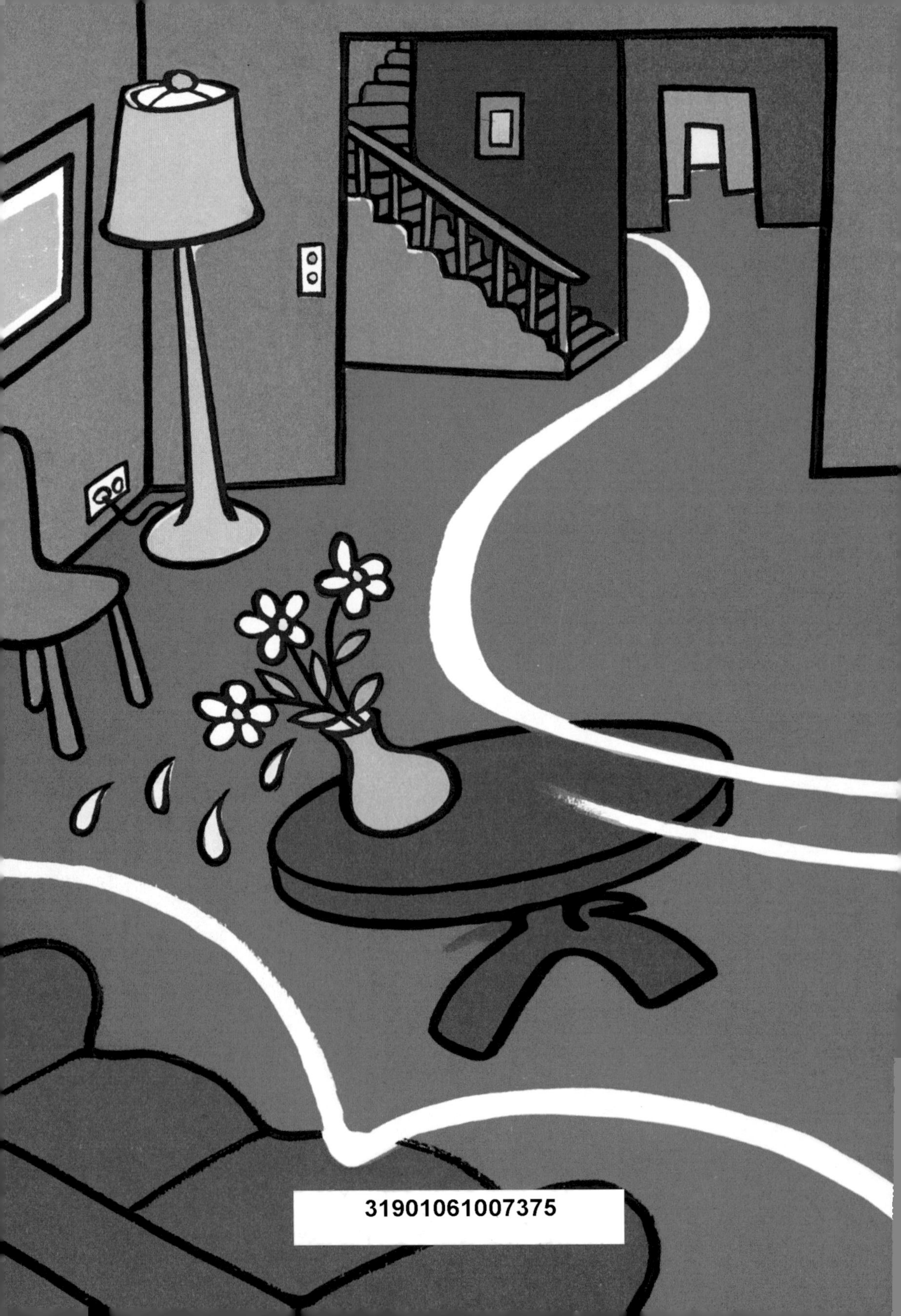